LIGHT LIFE LOVE

Lincoln Theological College
Passiontide Lecturers 1951–66

1951	H. E. W. TURNER	*The Atonement in Patristic Thought*
1952	MICHAEL RAMSEY	
1953	H. A. HODGES	*The Pattern of Atonement**
1954	R. P. SYMONDS	*Holy Week Liturgy*
1955	G. EVERY S.S.M.	*Lamb to the Slaughter*
1956	J. E. L. OULTON	*Mystery of the Cross*
1957	ULLRICH SIMON	*Suffering in the O.T.*
1958	F. W. DILLISTONE	*Atonement interpreted by Novelists**
1959	A. FARRER	*The Temptations*
1960	K. J. WOOLLCOMBE	*Epistle to the Hebrews*
1961	C. F. EVANS	*Passion Narratives*
1963	G. W. H. LAMPE	*The Atonement*
1964	HUGH MONTEFIORE	*Awkward Questions on Christian Love**
1965	S. BARRINGTON-WARD	*Atonement*
1966	A. A. K. GRAHAM	*The Sacraments*

* These Lectures have been published. Lecturers before 1951 included: CHARLES WILLIAMS; A. G. HERBERT; W. J. PAYTHIAN ADAMS; ROGER LLOYD.

LIGHT LIFE LOVE

The Passiontide Lectures for 1967
at Lincoln Theological College

The Holy Week Lectures for 1967
at Cuddesdon College, Oxford

by

W. NORMAN PITTENGER

King's College, Cambridge, and formerly
Professor of Christian Apologetics, General Theological Seminary, New York

LONDON
A. R. MOWBRAY & CO LTD

© A. R. Mowbray & Co Ltd 1967

Printed in Great Britain by
A. R. Mowbray & Co Ltd in the City of Oxford
74385

First published in 1967

Contents

ACKNOWLEDGEMENTS

THE thanks of the author and publishers are due to the following for permission to quote extracts:

The Cambridge University Press, *Adventure of Ideas* by A. N. Whitehead; Faber & Faber Ltd., *Four Quartets* by T. S. Eliot; Michael Joseph Ltd., *Another Country* by James Baldwin.

Preface

THE five chapters in this book were delivered as the Passiontide Lectures at Lincoln Theological College and the Holy Week Lectures at Cuddesdon College, Oxford, during March 1967. They are printed exactly as they were given.

It is difficult to know precisely what subject will be appropriate in such places on such occasions. Should one conduct a theological enquiry, or offer a series of devotional meditations, or speak of the 'practical application' of the doctrine of the Cross? I suppose that these five lectures could be classified under any one of these heads; but my intention was to do something in respect to all of them.

It remains to thank the Reverend Alan Webster, Principal of Lincoln, for his invitation to give the lectures in the first instance, and for his gracious consent to their repetition at Cuddesdon the following week; and to thank both him and the Reverend Robert Runcie, Principal of Cuddesdon, for their hospitality during the days spent in their respective colleges. For one who but recently has come to work in Britain after over thirty years of teaching, and living, in a theological college in the United States, it has been very pleasent to share in the life of these two notable schools for the training of men for the ministry of Christ's Holy Church.

King's College   NORMAN PITTENGER
Cambridge

1

The Man in whom God acted once-for-all

IT has often been said that Anglican theology is primarily a theology of the Incarnation, finding its centre and main point of concern in the person of Jesus Christ as Word-made-flesh, and giving little attention to the Atonement or the work of Christ in the redemption of sinful men. I do not believe that this statement, however frequently it has been made and whatever authority may be claimed for those who make it, is, in fact, accurate. Indeed one might say that those who talk in this way cannot have read with any thoroughness the corpus of Anglican divinity from the 1530s to the present day.

Doubtless from the publication of *Lux Mundi*, in the latter part of the last century, there has been a very considerable stress among Anglicans on what that celebrated symposium called 'the religion of the Incarnation'. Doubtless Anglicans have done a good deal of work, theologically, in studying the patristic development towards Chalcedon and in attempting various kinds of re-statement or re-conception of the doctrine of the person of Christ. But one has only to read the miscellaneous writings of our earliest Anglican divines in the time of Cranmer, or even the works of the Carolines, or the responsible leaders of the evangelical revival, or even the early Tractarians, to see that these thinkers did *not* neglect the Atonement, nor did they minimize what they would have called 'the exceeding sinfulness of man' and his need of redemption.

Even Hooker, who has been said to write *con amore* only in the *Fifth Book of the Ecclesiastical Polity* when he comes to discuss the Church in the light of the Incarnation, is under no illusions about man's condition and situation and does not speak of the Incarnation as if it had nothing to do with sin and redemption. Nor is it possible to read Frederick Denison Maurice, or his teacher and idol Samuel Taylor Coleridge, without recognizing that here too Atonement is by no means neglected or put in a secondary place in the total 'organism' of Christian faith.

What is to be observed, I think, is that Anglicans have quite consistently declined to talk about Atonement *in isolation from Incarnation*. Their line has been very much like that taken recently by the Scots-American theologian, George S. Hendry, whose moving book *The Gospel of the Incarnation* might be summarized as a sustained plea for the setting of the atoning work of Christ in the context of the total incarnate life of the Lord. Unlike Lutheran theology, for example, Anglicans have been convinced that whatever our Lord may have done for man by his death on Calvary, this can be understood only as the summing-up and completion of what in his entire life among us was being accomplished. The point of the medieval saying *tota vita Christi mysterium crucis* (the whole life of Christ is the mystery of the cross) has been their emphasis; and while they have not been so ready to concentrate on Calvary to the exclusion of Bethlehem and Nazareth, they have been quite ready to say, indeed to insist, that the question of the person of Christ—that is, a consideration of the Incarnation of God in the Man Jesus—arises for us only because of the totality of 'the benefits' of Christ. In other words, they have understood that we are interested in *who* Jesus is because we have experienced *what* Jesus does, but they have refused to separate the latter from the former and have quite consistently, and in my judgement rightly, declined to create a *theologia crucis* which did not involve and demand a *theologia incarnationis*.

Furthermore, the willingness of some continental theologians to let go the whole issue of the 'historical Jesus', granted only that one can be assured of the giving of authentic life by response to the gospel of the cross, has seemed to most Anglican divines to be a tragic reduction of the full truth of the Christian's faith. Indeed, they would say, one must respond in faith and self-surrender to the cross, or rather to the person whose 'willingness to die' constituted (as St. Bernard said) the real sacrifice which was offered once-for-all. At the same time, they would maintain, the person who died is in fact the person who lived among us as a Man among men, sharing our common lot, knowing our common experience, participating in the vicissitudes of our common life; and it is only when we know something of the kind of person it was who thus lived among us, that we can understand what he accomplished for us, by his total life, and focally and supremely by his offering of himself in death according to what he took to be the will of the God whom he had served and revealed in all that preceded the events 'outside the city wall'.

Again, it has also been said that Anglican divinity is strongly christocentric—obviously this assertion is linked with the notion, which I hope to have shown to be mistaken, that the Incarnation is the chief concern of our theology. To this charge of christocentricity, we must reply that it too rests upon a very selective reading of Anglican theological works. Of course it is true that because of the strong emphasis on the person and work of

Christ as our central clue to the nature of God, Anglican
divinity has devoted much time and attention to the
significance of our Lord, always or nearly always (as I
have insisted) in the light of his 'benefits'; but it is simply
not the case that Anglican theologians have failed to be
vigorously theocentric in their attempt to understand the
faith by which they live. Unlike that excessive attention
to the person of Christ sometimes found in other post-
Reformation traditions—whether by a liberal Protestant
concentration on the Jesus of history or a neo-orthodox
concentration on the Christ of faith—Anglican divinity
has been more ready to talk of *God* incarnate in Christ, or
of the accomplishment wrought for men by *God* through
the person and work of Christ, or of the revelation of the
nature of *God* in the manhood of Jesus. Thus Paul van
Buren's centring of all attention, in his book *The Secular
Meaning of the Gospel*, on the life of Jesus and 'the historical
perspective' associated with that life, with the rejection of
talk about the God who sent Jesus (which surely is the
New Testament, and, above all, the gospel emphasis), is
a-typical of Anglican divinity. Van Buren's years of
study with Barth are reflected in his christocentrism,
although Barth himself would never for a moment think
it possible to make Jesus as 'the free man for others' the
whole point of Christian faith, with nothing said about
that manhood as the revelatory instrument for the Word
of God and hence for the one and only true God himself.
It is really a little difficult to see why charges of christocentrism have been made against Anglicanism, when at
the same time it has been alleged that Anglican theologians
have been altogether too much interested in the metaphysical consequences of Christian faith, or have been
far too ready to understand the person of Christ in the

light of a total world-view which is the context for, and
the final point of, the claims made about the Lord.

I have made this kind of defence of Anglican theology,
I hope not proudly or arrogantly or with the appearance
of claiming that everything Anglican is sound and true,
but because in this course of lectures during Passion and
Holy Week I wish to speak of God's revelation in act, or
the activity which reveals God, seen in our Christian faith
as finding its focus, or what von Hügel once called 'its
implied goal and centre', in the Man Jesus and in what
God is believed to have 'determined, dared, and done' in
that place and through that person. I believe that what I
am doing here is entirely in accord with the main trend
of Anglican divinity, both because I shall be speaking of
the 'benefits' of Christ only in relation to his whole life
and of his person only in relation to his supreme achievement, and also because I shall be setting all this in the
context of a philosophical world-view which I believe
to be viable for us today in a world that is a dynamic,
moving, directive process.

On many occasions, and indeed in several books, I
have quoted the memorable words once written by Professor Alfred North Whitehead about what he calls 'the
supreme moment in religious history, according to the
Christian religion'. Here is the quotation, from page 214
of the original Cambridge University Press edition of
Adventures of Ideas (1933): 'The essence of Christianity is
the appeal to the life of Christ as a revelation of the nature
of God and of his agency in the world. The record is
fragmentary, inconsistent, and uncertain. It is not
necessary for me to express any opinion as to the proper
reconstruction of the most likely tale of historic fact.
Such a procedure would be useless, without value, and

entirely out of place in this book. But there can be no
doubt as to what elements in the record have evoked a
response from all that is best in human nature. The
Mother, the Child, and the bare manger: the lowly man,
homeless and self-forgetful, with his message of peace,
love, and sympathy: the suffering, the agony, the tender
words as life ebbed, the final despair: and the whole with
the authority of supreme victory.'

Having written this magnificent paragraph, Whitehead
went on to note: 'Can there be any doubt that the power
of Christianity lies in its revelation in act, of that which
Plato divined in theory?' What was it that Plato had
divined 'in theory'? For Whitehead it was just this, as he
put it on the preceding page of his book: 'that the
divine element in the world is to be conceived as a per-
suasive agency and not as a coercive agency'. This was
Plato's 'final conviction', we are told; it is one of 'the
greatest intellectual discoveries in the history of religion';
'it is plainly enunciated by Plato, although he failed to
co-ordinate it systematically with the rest of his metaphysical theory'. And for Whitehead the alternative
position, which regards 'God as the supreme agency of
compulsion', is utterly impossible in its assumption that
God is 'omnipotently disposing a wholly derivative
world'—a world, that is, which makes no contribution on
its part to the divine life and can be but the passive
recipient of the activity of 'the final coercive forces' in the
structure of things.

My concern here, of course, is not with the metaphysics
of Whitehead, although in honesty to myself and in
fairness to you I must confess that I find that metaphysics,
suitably adapted and ordered, satisfactory to my mind
and responsive to the deep needs of my heart. What I

am concerned with doing is to show that the Passion of
Christ, summing up and as it were placarding before us
the total impression of Jesus which the gospel narratives
afford us, is in fact the disclosure, in terms which we men
can grasp and *be grasped by*, of 'the nature of God and
his agency in the world'. It manifests *in act* what God is
and what God is up to in this world. It is not in utter and
stark opposition to the world, as if it were a solitary,
un-related, intrusion 'from without' into the going-on of
things; but it is a vivid exposition, in concrete human
historical terms, of the deepest and highest truth in that
going-on; and precisely because it is such an exposition, it
corrects our cheaper, easier, more sentimental and comfortable ideas, while at the same time it provides both a
vision of what truly *is* the case and also affords the enabling strength which impels us to fashion our own lives
and the world of men about us, after the pattern of that
true vision.

It is my plan to develop this theme under three heads,
suggested to me by words familiar to us from the Fourth
Gospel. First, we shall speak of *Light*—the illumination
which the Lord of this holy season gives us about God
and ourselves. Then we shall speak of *Life*—the empowering which theology calls 'grace' and which, following the
teaching of John Oman, we may venture to think of in
terms of the enormous strength of personal influence as
this is brought to bear upon our lives. Finally, we shall
speak of *Love*—the light which Christ brings and the life
which he imparts give us the assurance that there is
compassion at the heart of creation, that 'God is love',
and that Love is both *God's* nature, 'his essence and his
very self', and the 'new nature' which he would enable
in us; it is the strongest thing, indeed the only truly

strong thing, in this or any other world. In the light of those three Christian convictions, given us by the total impression of our Lord's existence among us and brought to focus by the events of his passion, death, and resurrection, we shall conclude by some discussion of what I take to be the fourth and undergirding conviction of all genuinely Christian faith and the necessary pre-condition for all genuinely Christian worship and action: namely, that Jesus Christ is what Whitehead would have described as 'important'.

Although this point must be developed in our conclusion, it is necessary to say something about it immediately, lest I be quite misunderstood. By 'importance', Whitehead means an occurrence, an event, in his own idiom some 'occasion', which is both objectively of a high order of significance in that it is related to, and serves as peculiar concentration for, the entire sequence of antecedent and accompanying events or occurrences or 'occasions', and also subjectively because it evokes from those who are in its presence a response of appreciation which includes not only the mind's consent but also the richer aesthetic or 'felt' reaction to something which we might describe as both wonderful and deeply moving. That which is 'important' illuminates the process of the past, puts in a vivid light that which is going on in the present, and opens up further and fuller possibilities of apprehension and of action in the future. The 'important' is the definitive and the decisive; it has about it a certain kind of uniqueness, but the uniqueness is what Professor Moule has lately taught us to call 'uniqueness of inclusion', not 'uniqueness of exclusion'. I take it to be the deepest conviction of Christian faith that in this sense Jesus is indeed 'important', in what he said and did, and in what was wrought out in and through and around him in his concrete and specific historicity.

That reference to 'concrete and specific historicity' brings me to the final point in this first lecture. I wish to say something about what seems to me the absolute necessity, for Christian faith, of some assurance concerning the 'Jesus of History', as he used to be called—that is, concerning the Man who lived in Palestine at a given time and place and under given circumstances and conditions.

Now I am not one of those who suppose that the demands of faith can create the certitudes of history. Just because we as Christians depend on some assurance concerning the history of Jesus, in the ordinary sense of that word, we dare not suppose that this need will give us the fact of the history; and I am deeply suspicious of the kind of approach to New Testament study that seems to think that such study must inevitably give us what our prior wishes might desire. On the other hand, I can see no reason to assume that the Christian faith, in anything like its traditional form, could survive for very long if it became quite clear that we know nothing about Jesus as an historical figure, or that what we know is so utterly vague and unclear that we cannot form any picture of him which will carry conviction and evoke response. But I am very sure that sane, even if radical, historical enquiry does *not* result in a demolition of the picture of Jesus as a Man among men. Even form-criticism in the manner of its extreme exponents need not lead to that conclusion; and I suspect that some of the more negative conclusions commonly ascribed to Bultmann (conclusions which other interpreters and Bultmann himself would indeed disavow, if I read them and him

B

rightly) are more the result of certain theological presuppositions than the consequence of historical enquiry. By this I mean that it is fairly certain that a scholar who is convinced, *ab initio*, that any appeal to history violates some refined version of the doctrine of justification by faith alone, may well be ready to push to extravagant limits the obvious uncertainties attaching to the details of Jesus' life and teaching; while a scholar who thinks that *all* history is quite unimportant, is likely to think that a sceptical attitude towards *any* historical event is almost invevitable.

It is interesting that in what nowadays is called 'the new quest for the historical Jesus' there is a willingness to use all the techniques of the form-critical method, as well as the older literary criticism, historical criticism, and history-of-religion procedures, without the assumption that nothing at all can be known of that 'historical figure. Indeed, in Bornkamm's movingly written *Jesus of Nazareth*, a close follower of Bultmann gives us what seems to me a very convincing historical portrait; and Bornkamm is but one of a number of continental scholars who refuse to subscribe to the supposed historical scepticism which is often thought to be the necessary consequence of all radical study of the New Testament. Professor John Knox, in a whole series of books, has made it plain that we do in fact know a great deal about Jesus, although we know what we know through the living memory of the community which 'remembers him, rather than by means of any biographical or journalistic— shall I say 'dictaphonic' and 'candid-camera'?—accounts.

But this is not the place nor have I here the time to enter upon an extended discussion of the situation in New Testament studies. I can only state my own position, based I hope on honest historical enquiry and marked I hope by some degree of common sense. I am convinced that what Professor Bethune-Baker, many years ago, in a little book called *Early Traditions about Jesus* (a book which is still of much value, although it has been forgotten in recent years), spoke of as the 'impressions of Jesus' which the gospel material provides for us, are very close indeed to the actual facts of the life of the Man who lived in Palestine nearly two thousand years ago. Of course we must read the 'impressions' with critical regard for the ways in which they come to us, and the ways in which they are recounted; of course there are many places where details are heightened or distorted; of course the teaching has been expanded or modified in this or that particular. We should expect this to be the case with any such collection of impressions. But what emerges from a careful, critical, and meditative reading of the material is the portait of a Man, a Man who can be described in such words as I quoted earlier from Whitehead: a Man with his message of peace, love, and sympathy; a Man who underwent experiences of suffering, agony, and despair; a Man whose 'tender words' were greatly cherished and never forgotten; a Man whose whole life had about it 'the authority of supreme victory'; and, what Whitehead did not say, a Man whose whole 'meat' was 'to do the will' of the God and Father who, he believed, had sent him.

Even if we may feel that the stories of the 'signs'—or what some would still wish to call, by a word hardly used in the gospels themselves, 'the miracles'—are impossible to accept in their particulars, we can yet have confidence, on strictly historical grounds, that such

stories testify vividly and movingly to the utterly enormous, indeed overwhelming, impression that Jesus made
upon those who companied with him. These stories are
among our most valuable pieces of material, not because
they are precise cinematographic reproductions of factual
occurrences, but because they show us the sort of Man
Jesus was, what he was in the experience of those who
were with him 'in the flesh', and what he was known to
be in the continuing fellowship with him through and
after his death on the Cross, in the 'community of the
resurrection' which was the primitive Christian Church.

For myself I should say that this historical reliability,
in the specific sense in which I am using the term, is as
much true of the Fourth Gospel as of the Synoptics.
Admittedly more meditative, admittedly more highly
theological, admittedly much concerned with the significance of Jesus as 'Word-made-flesh', the Fourth Gospel
yet rests back, I am sure (and here I am grateful to the
work of Dr. Gardner-Smith, Dr. C. H. Dodd, and the
Bishop of Woolwich), upon genuinely historical traditions
different from but not utterly alien to the traditions
which are given us in the first three gospels.

Do we know Jesus? Yes, I think, we *do* know him; we
know him *very well*; we know him in the really important
way of knowing about any historical personage. That is,
we know him in how he was remembered by those who
themselves knew him. Complete scepticism seems to me
not only absurd, but impossible. It is not that the demands
of Christian faith create the figure they would like to
adore; rather it is that the methods of sound historical
enquiry, such as would be employed in respect to any
person in the past, provide us with a reliable picture,
although of course not a facsimile photograph, of him in

whom Christian faith finds the light which illuminates us, the life which empowers us, and the love which assures us—him in whom, as a true Man living a genuinely human life, God acted to reveal himself, in unparalleled intimacy and with supreme adequacy, as what Whitehead called 'the divine persuasion'. Or in the more familiar words of our Christian heritage: 'God is Love'; and this we believe because 'God loved us, and sent his Son', in whom we see him at work with unmistakable clarity and extraordinary power.

2

Christ who brings Light

WHEN I was a young man I was privileged to enjoy the
friendship of Paul Elmer More, the distinguished literary
critic and classicist, whose collected essays entitled
Shelburne Essays and whose study of Platonism and Christian faith called *The Greek Tradition* ought not to have
been forgotten or neglected. More had been converted
to Christianity in middle-age because to him it seemed
that the fulfilment of the Greek philosophical and moral
quest was to be found in the person of Jesus Christ; he
became a devout, if somewhat unconventional, Anglican.
One day we were speaking of the gospels and of the less
than perfect Greek in which they are written; and More
remarked, 'But surely no one can read the Passion stories,
and particularly that of Mark, without tears.' He went
on to point out that he had always been moved by the
breathless quality of Mark's style and added, 'In the
Marcan Passion narrative, you have the sense of Jesus
going through the events which are recorded, not as
their victim but as the triumphant victor.'

Surely this is true. As we read of our Lord's going up
to Jerusalem, his last days in the city with his disciples
and the people, his conversations with the Jewish religious
leaders, the Last Supper in the upper room, the Garden
of Gethsemane, the arrest and trial, the way of the Cross
to Golgotha, the final moments as he approached death,

14

and the death itself, we do not have the feeling that we are watching one who is tossed to and fro by circumstance. On the contrary, the impression that the narratives give—and as More said, especially St. Mark's—is of mastery and lordship. We are told earlier that 'he set his face to go up to Jerusalem'; but I think we have a sense of Jesus' 'setting his face to go' through all the events which the gospels record in their concluding chapters. In the Garden of Gethsemane, when the temptation to disobey what seemed God's purpose was strong upon him, it was rejected most certainly and decisively; and surely we should read the words of self-surrender with the emphasis in a different place from that commonly given them when they are read in the lessons in public worship: 'Not my will, but thine *be done.*' Jesus does not accept God's will in some passive acquiescence in a ghastly fate; he accepts it as if he were saying, 'Thy will, O Father, *must* be done; and let it *be* done through *me.*' Here is an eager if painful identification of his human will with what he believed to be the Father's will; and here too is an eager desire that the Father's will should be done—as the Epistle to the Hebrews rightly discerns, he was come to do the Father's will and he accepted it with *joy*, even though the doing of it meant for him suffering and death.

Such an interpretation is confirmed when the Fourth Evangelist puts in the mouth of the Crucified the great phrase: 'It is finished.' For, as we all know, this phrase does not mean, in the Greek, simply the completion of an imposed task which has been accepted reluctantly and sadly. It is a great cry of triumph: 'What I came to do is now *accomplished.*' The victim is the mighty victor; he has fulfilled his given task and there is a note of wonderful joy in the achievement. So it is that we are not to read

our Lord's passion and death with a feeling of pity, as if
we were thinking, 'Poor chap, it was an awful fate, but
he bore it bravely'. We are to read it with a sense of the
triumph of the will of God in the life of man; the story is
told, as I have quoted from Whitehead, 'with the authority
of supreme victory'. The early church understood this
much better than the medieval Church and even the
common Christian attitude in our own day; to this fact
the hymns of Venantius Fortunatus give witness: 'The
royal banners forward go. . . .' 'God is reigning from the
Tree. . . .' There is in those hymns a moving tenderness,
but there is no maudlin sentimentality, no expression of
pity; rather, there is a feeling of the triumph of Jesus not
only after but on the cross. This is indeed 'earth's darkest
hour', but the darkness is shot through with the glory of
conquest.

Shot through with the glory of conquest . . . yes, and the
glory is the light which Christ both is in himself and brings
to us who call ourselves by his name. He is the 'light of
the world', we say, and nowhere is that light more manifest than in what might appear to be utter blackness. This
is the strange paradox of Christian faith as it contemplates
its Lord.

Christ, then, is the light-bringer. What does this light
reveal to us? To an answer to this question we shall now
turn.

First of all, something is disclosed to us about ourselves.
If we are indeed those for whom Christ died, if he cared
enough to do this, then no man dare think of himself as
worthless, useless, hopeless. All through the story of
Jesus we find him assuring those whom he met that they
were of value—of value in his eyes and of value in the
sight of his heavenly Father. The despised tax-collector,

the woman who was a sinner, the little children whom he took in his arms: these are but a few of the many to whom he was able to give this reassuring self-understanding. In the last days of his earthly life, the same is seen. Those who arrested him and brought him to trial, those who condemned him and crucified him, those who were beside him on their crosses, were neither denounced nor derided. They were seen as men, as the children of God, and respected as such.

It seems to me that far too much Christian piety has felt that the only proper way to think of ourselves is as creatures beyond all possibility of recovery. Bonhoeffer, in his protest against what he had known of a certain kind of religiosity, insisted that it was unworthy of a Christian to attempt to *put* himself in that state of utter despair to which the offer of redemption might then speak. I am sure that he was right. The sort of 'vermiform' view of ourselves which seems to characterize a good deal of our Anglican liturgy is not genuinely Christian. We are indeed sinners, but the continual dwelling upon what miserable creatures we are is unhealthy and morbid. The gospel is not a desperate expedient to get us out of our given manhood; it is the way of restoration to the manhood which is ours by God's act in creating us. Each of us knows how seriously he has damaged that manhood; each of us knows that all is not well with him; each of us knows that he has 'fallen' from the intention which God has for him. But the way in which a Christian comes to know all this is by the contemplation of the sheer love of God in Jesus Christ, which shames him into an acknowledgement of his defection; we ought not to expect or engage in a continual harping on our dirtiness and the evil of our ways. Nor should we allow ourselves to pursue what von Hügel so amusingly but so accurately described as 'a spiritual flea-hunt'. Our sin will be quite plain to us if we only *look:* look first at the crucified Lord and then at ourselves.

And the fact remains that even in and with our sin, we are still made in the image of God. That image has been damaged, dirtied, denied: yes, but never utterly shattered. For God, who is greater than our minds and our hearts, is greater also than our sinning; and his loving creation of us with the intention that we shall be his faithful sons still stands secure. It is he, and he only, who knows the secrets of our hearts and the muddied state of our lives—he knows them much better than we do ourselves; and yet he loves us. We are unworthy of his love, but we are unfailingly the children of that love. So, as it seems to me, Christ assures us of our value in God's scheme and of the yearning of God that we shall become what he would have us to be. Hopelessness, despair, morbid dwelling upon what wretches we are, will never do us any good. What it will do is centre our theology on ourselves and not on God; it will turn our religious practice sour and inhuman; and it will make our relationships with others unpleasant and unattractive. Can *that* be Christian?

In the second place, the light of Christ reveals to us the truth about our human contacts and relationships. It is possible to regard our fellows as if they were there only to be exploited by us. It is also possible to think of them and act towards them as if they were curiosities to be explored, as a scientist might examine and observe some natural phenomenon or some behaviour-pattern. But from Jesus we learn that the attitude which we are to take towards others and the relationship which we are

have with them, is to be characterized by acceptance
nd understanding, compassion and sympathy. This
eed not mean a sloppy indifference to wrongs where
hey exist, nor need it lead us to an easy acquiescence in
nything they may think or do. A recent writer in the
tates has said that we are called upon to be 'fools for
Christ's sake', but not 'damned fools'. He has illustrated
he point by remarking that the 'damned fool' is the one
who has no discrimination, no principle, no standard, in
erms of which he understands himself and tries to
connect' with others. A 'fool for Christ's sake' is one who
nows that we are all knit together in that 'bundle of
fe' of which the Old Testament writer speaks. Hence
we are to have a deep fellow-feeling, a compassion, for
others; we are to look for the best in them, not the worst;
we are to open ourselves to them rather than close ourselves
against them.

This surely is seen in our Lord throughout his ministry
nd supremely in his attitude and action in the last days.
The supreme example, I suppose, is found in the story of
he penitent robber and Jesus' acceptance of him. I
hink it is also found in the other robber, whom Jesus did
ot condemn or denounce, so far as the story goes, but
accepted even in his impenitence, for Jesus did not have
o speak in order to care. Nor do we. A good deal of the
ime it is by what we do *not* say that we can best exhibit
our compassionate understanding. For myself, I come
more and more to the conviction that it is by a passive
activity that we best show our loving; by this I mean that
words, words, words' are not the way always to relate
ourselves to others in deep concern and caring.

Years ago I heard from an old lady that a certain
parson whom I knew was for her the supreme case of

understanding compassion. It turned out that when sh
was a young woman, that clergyman had come to th
house where her father was dying. He had remaine
with the family a whole night, until death finally cam
He had not said a word, for he knew that the famil
were not practising Christians. But he had been *ther*
with them and for them; and they knew it. Often,
think, the clergy talk too much, when what is needed an
wanted is simple sharing of an experience in lovin
silence. What is true for the parson is true for all Chris
tians: the relationship which our Lord reveals to us i
his whole life with us, and in his death for us, is one c
identification, of fellow-living with others.

In the third place, the light of Christ reveals to us
when Calvary is seen in the glory of resurrection, tha
the very world itself is with us and for us. Certainly i
does not *look* that way. St. Thomas Aquinas begins hi
discussion of God's existence with some strange words: *a
deus sit? videtur non.* 'Is there a God? It does not seem so
That is profoundly realistic; and we shall get nowhere i
we deny or neglect the countless bits of evidence whic
appear to make it absurd to think that there is a purpos
of good, a heart of love, in and behind what much of th
time seems a terrible and terrifying world. Yet the con
viction of the Christian, contemplating the events c
Passiontide and Holy Week and seeing them in the know
ledge of the 'supreme victory' which was placarded befor
us on Easter Day, is that the secret of the world is ther
laid bare. Despite everything that seems to say 'No'
the Christian must then and with utter confidence sa
'Yes'.

The light of Christ does not suggest a rosy optimism
which, after the fashion of Mary Baker Eddy and he

ollowers, shuts its eyes to the evil in the world. Perhaps George Tyrrell was nearer the truth when he said that he Christian was a pessimist in respect to proximate hings and an optimist in respect to ultimate things: yet should prefer to say that the Christian is a *realist*, who ecognizes evil for what it is but who knows also that the Love which is God is triumphant over that evil. 'He makes even the wrath of man to turn to his praise'; Calvary is the visible enactment of the Psalmist's conviction about God. Not only man's wrath, however, but all manner of evil wherever found: all this can be absorbed by God and used in strange and wonderful ways as occasion for good. Thus in the light brought by Christ we can walk confidently and gladly in this world, knowing that it is neither a mad-house nor a prison, but the Father's creation, where 'not a sparrow falls to the ground without your Father' and where the worst that can happen, as Bonhoeffer himself wrote to his friend, can become the means by which 'joy and peace in believing' is made possible for us.

Finally, the light of Christ is the light of God; and 'in that light we see light' in God himself. 'God is light and in him is no darkness at all', the Johannine writer tells us. I take it that he means that God is indeed mysterious but not unpredictable or subject to change of attitude or mood. The whole of the Old Testament is concerned to declare God's abiding faithfulness; his children can *count on him*. And the New Testament assures us that his faithfulness is his unswerving purpose of love. That love may be expressed in ways that surprise us, but it will never become something else. 'Is God a man, that he should change his mind?' No. God is the God whose character has been disclosed, whose ways in the world are all of a piece, whose purpose is made plain in the revelation which he has given of himself.

There are many bits of our common Christian practice which need correction, if this be true. I take but one, to illustrate the point. All too frequently in our prayer, we seem to suppose that God can be persuaded to give us what we think we want; we indulge in a sort of wrangling with him, hoping to get him on our side. Yet surely prayer which has understood that God is what Christ shows him to be—in other words, prayer in the light which Christ brings—will be prayer that trusts God to do good even if the good is not what we might have expected. In the present moment and in the future, God will give us 'more than we can desire', provided our desire is for that which God purposes. The classical definition of prayer found first I think in St. John Damascene, and repeated by St. Thomas Aquinas, is 'the elevation of the mind to God'. Nowhere in the great masters of Christian spirituality does one find a description of prayer which would suggest that God cannot be trusted to do the best unless we inform him what he ought to do.

Our Lord commended himself and all that he was and was doing to the Father's hands, in the sure confidence that it was safe in those hands. He trusted God and committed himself in that trust. The whole life of our Lord was like that: it was a perfect trust in God and it was all an act of prayer. The moments on the mountain, the special occasions of which we get little glimpses now and again in the gospels, when Jesus retired for a time to 'pray to the Father who seeth in secret', were of a piece with his life. And in Gethesmane, the prayer which he offered was exactly the prayer which his whole life had been praying: that the Father's will should be done. So it should be with us. Our practice of prayer and our teaching about it should have as its centre the faithfulness of God, his unfailing will of love, his desire for the good of all men; if you will let me put it so, the utterly indiscriminate character of his love which is not an indiscriminate acquiesence in anything that happens but an indiscriminate concern that the best shall be brought into the lives of all men. God is 'sheer unbounded love'; he is not 'choosey' or 'chancey'. He *cares*.

So we come full-circle. For if *God* cares, we must care also. 'If God so loved us, ought we not also to love one another'? Which means, I think, that Christian activity in any area of the human enterprise is marked by that love, that caring. Doubtless some of you are thinking that I speak far too much about God as Love. But I cannot do otherwise, for I am convinced that this is the central truth of our faith, overshadowed in much theology by other interests and concerns and sometimes forgotten when God is thought to be chiefly power or might. Professor Whitehead once said that 'God is the fellow-sufferer who understands'. If that be patripassianism, I do not mind. I am sure that it is *true*. In the light which streams from Calvary we ought to know it to be true, although that light also assures us that the 'fellow-sufferer' is the triumphant one whose real omnipotence rests in the profound reality of a love that 'never faileth'.

The light which is Christ is also 'the life of men'. It is to a discussion of Christ as that life that we shall turn in our next lecture. But I conclude this one with the familiar words of T. S. Eliot, as he describes this world of

ours and ourselves in it when they are seen in the light
which is Christ:

> The whole earth is our hospital
> Endowed by the ruined millionaire,
> Wherein, if we do well, we shall
> Die of the absolute paternal care
> That will not leave us, but prevents us everywhere.[1]

[1] 'East Coker' in *Four Quartets*, by T. S. Eliot.

3

Christic who brings Life

KIERKEGAARD often spoke of Jesus as the pattern but he was profoundly aware of the centrality of our Lord as power. So it is that we must move from Christ as the revealer of the truth about ourselves, our fellowmen, our world, and God himself, to Christ as that one in whom life—new life, 'eternal life', as the Johannine writer would say—is made available for men.

The point of Christian faith is not that Jesus merely discloses the truth; rather, it is that Jesus embodies and enacts the truth: 'to do the truth' is more profound than simply to know it or to show it. In this respect, the whole biblical witness provides a background for Jesus as the doer of the truth and hence as himself the bringer of life. For the scriptures are quite clear that God is the living God, who enters into nature and history unceasingly and unfailingly, working out a purpose that is for the good of all creation. In the Old Testament God does not remain aloof from his world; neither is he the 'unmoved mover' who once acted but now lets things go on without his energizing presence and operation. One of the continuing problems in Christian theology has been the reconciliation of static concepts of God and the world with the dynamic symbols that are found in the Bible; t would have been better to have let the latter modify, ndeed utterly change, the former, instead of allowing the biblical symbols to be lost in a philosophical framework

which often was in serious contradiction to them. If
it has done nothing else, the revival of what is styled
'biblical theology' in our time has forced us to reckon
much more radically with this dynamic portrayal and
to refuse any longer to be bogged down in a metaphysic
that cannot do justice to the biblical witness.

But if God is the God who is everlastingly present in
action in his world, and if Jesus is the one in whom the
truth is enacted and done, then we may regard our
Lord as the bringer of the life which is of God, which
in fact is God's life in man. And it is brought to us by
the gracious influence of his presence and the invigorating
strength of his relationship with us, as our brother man.
Bishop Kirk used to define 'grace' in St. Augustine's
writings as meaning 'God's love in action'; it is precisely
this which communicates life to us in the specifically
Christian sense.

Of course we are not here speaking of biological life,
nor are we asserting that apart from Jesus and his grace
there is no sharing whatever in the life of God in the
world. It should be unthinkable for a Christian theist
to talk as if the *only* channel for divine life, whereby we
are made 'partakers in the divine nature' (as 2 Peter has
it), is the Jesus of history or the Christ known in explicitly
Christian faith. The traditional doctrine of the Logos
or Word of God germinally present in every man ought
to guard us against that error. On the other hand
there is a new *quality* of life which comes in and through
Jesus Christ; it is a specifically Christian life, in fact it
is 'life in Christ' in the familiar Pauline phrase, with
which we are here concerned. I should wish to characterize that quality of life by calling it true or authentic,
strongly purposive, genuinely empowering, courageous,

and marked throughout by the kind of love-in-action which is seen exhibited, enacted, *done* in the whole story of Jesus and supremely in his crucifixion and resurrection. Let us speak of each of these points.

Among young people in the United States, the supreme word of contempt in recent years has been 'phoney'. J. D. Salinger's *Catcher in the Rye* was the novel that caught this expression of contempt, as American youth employed it, and firmly fixed its meaning for us elders. A phoney play was a play that did not ring true; a phoney book was a book that cheaply misrepresented the facts of experience; a phoney person, sometimes described simply as 'a phoney', was someone who lacked the quality of authenticity, who played a role which was not really his, who pretended to be what he was not, who 'put on an act' without being heart-and-soul engaged in it. The opposite of a phoney person, then, is someone who is 'above-board', as they say in the States, whose life and actions 'ring true', who does not pretend to be what he is not, who in a word is authentically a man. May I suggest to you that Jesus Christ, in the stories we read about him, is *never* 'a phoney', is always an authentic man? About what he says, what he does, how he acts and how he re-acts, there is utter authenticity. Here is a committed man, who in giving himself entirely and without reserve to that which commands him—namely, the righteous and loving will of his heavenly Father—establishes, in his total existence as a man, a kind of absolute integrity. It is worth our noting that while a great many people turn from the Church and dismiss the Christian enterprise as ridiculous or outworn, the figure of Jesus himself never fails to receive their respect and even reverence; and I think that the reason for this is that such people

sense about him the truth, the authenticity, of his man
hood. The Fourth Gospel has a word for it: *aletheia*
Aletheia means genuine reality, utter integrity, openness
and naked honesty. This is *the* Man. *Ecce homo*: yes
in him not only Pilate but millions of others have seen
and still do see, authentic manhood.

Jesus does not pretend; he speaks the truth because he
knows the truth and because he does the truth; and thi
has led those who have long contemplated his figure to
call him *the* Truth. But in him the truth is not somethin
that is beheld; it is something that is done. It is *livin*
truth. He does not equivocate, he does not hide behind
excuses, he goes through his entire life and most notabl
what met him during his last days in Jerusalem, with
kind of honesty in him which made even his enemies fee
genuine awe in his presence. But the truth which he live
is not kept for himself. The imitation of Christ, by whic
I mean the letting of his self-giving enter into our ow
existence, leads us equally to be true men. The truth whic
is in him sets *us* free; pretence is no longer necessary, lie
will no longer be attractive, hiding is no longer possible
The life of the man in Christ begins, perhaps very diml
but as time goes on increasingly, to reflect something c
that integrity—and the integrity, the authenticity, produce
a courage to which we shall return shortly. 'Men too
notice of them, that they had been with Jesus.'

In the second place, among the illustrative points tha
we have selected for discussion of the meaning of the li
of Christ as shared with his people, we must speak c
purpose. In Jesus himself this is entirely plain. 'M
meat is to do the will of him that sent me.' The purpos
which dominated his entire career was alignment of h
human will with that of his Father; hence all that h

lid was to be in accord with God's holy will. His satisfaction was not in anything less than that. It is, I suppose,
possible that in those last days, Jesus might have found
an escape from obedience to that will; but having 'set
his face to go up to Jerusalem', he proceeded to act in
complete conformity with what he took to be the pur-
posed goal of his human existence. The purpose of this
Man was identified with the purpose of God for him.
That is why he was so free, even when he was nailed to
the Cross. For his acceptance of the Father's purpose
turned what might have been only fate into an intended
and fruitful destiny.

We do not know exactly how Jesus understood that
purpose for the record is somewhat confused, and there
are various ways in which New Testament scholars have
interpreted such evidence as there is: Did he understand
the purpose as messianic? Was his role that of the
prophet? Did he see the Father's will as simple obedience
and leave the results and the names entirely open?
Whatever may be the answer to these and similar ques-
tions, the fact remains that here is a life centred in a
purpose that was most firmly and unshakably taken to
be God's purpose. Life without some unifying purpose
is life in chaos; the life of Jesus was an ordered life, an
unified life, in which each action undertaken, each word
spoken, each relationship shared, played its part in working
out some aspect or portion of the over-arching end which
was before him.

Professor Whitehead has spoken of the 'subjective aim'
which gives direction to each actual entity as the series of
occasions of which it is the routing or movement emerge
and make their contribution and then pass away. He
has also said that the end of each entity is the 'satisfaction'

of that aim, the fulfilling of it and the bringing of it into actual expression—an expression which is then shared with other entities in a constant process of enrichment and growth. I should like to apply this set of ideas to the picture of Jesus in the gospels. Here the 'subjective aim' is the doing of the will of God which is the enhancement of all human life through the release of love into the word. Here the events which occur are all contributory to the fulfilment of that aim. Here the final 'satisfaction' is fulfilment of such an order that not only is Jesus himself recognized for what he really is, but there is an opening through him of new possibilities for others, the creation in them of new capacities for enhanced life in love, in fellowship with others, and in the establishment of a society in which love is the continuing social aim. So Jesus, we may say, accomplished through the 'aim' which was his, the purpose of God for him and in him: 'he saw of the travail of his soul' and, as we must affirm, 'he was satisfied'.

For those who are his followers, there is given a purposive life. The way in which human life can be lived, centred in an aim that fulfils and is fulfilling, is not only exhibited; it is imparted. Once again, the strange kind of influence which we call 'grace' is at work. Jesus' purpose becomes our purpose as we let ourselves be drawn to him in his own accomplishment of the purpose which was his. Life which has direction and meaning becomes a possibility; it even becomes a realized thing—and I suppose that is what sanctity really comes to. 'Purity of heart', Kierkegaard told us, 'is to will one thing': and the one thing willed in him who was altogether pure of heart was 'the will of him that sent him'. Our 'purity of heart', likewise, is the willing of the 'one thing', which

for us has been declared in the life, death, and victory of
Jesus our Lord.

But as we have seen, this is not only exhibited; it is
imparted. So the life in Christ, like the life of Jesus himself, is the empowered life. A Scots divine once wrote of
'the expulsive power of a new affection'; in Jesus there
has been provided for us a centre not only of loyalty but
also of love, which we dare to trust unreservedly. Hence,
from that loyalty in love and love in loyalty, an 'expulsive
power' is generated. It is power in the midst of ordinary
life, not power to escape from that life. It is an enabling
of human personality which makes men triumphant in
pain and suffering, in war and conflict, in sickness and
at death, as well as in the glad moments of their lives.
It is 'grace', as we say; and I remind you again that
'grace' means 'God's love in action', in action even in
such poor specimens of manhood as you and I. In our
Lord himself we see the gracious working of God which
strengthened him to face all that happened to him, without whining, without complaint, without retreat. He
was enabled to carry through to the end . . . and I see no
reason why, if we grant the full reality of Jesus' manhood,
we should not say of him what St. Paul said of himself:
'not I, but the grace of God which was with me'. That
grace which is love-in-action, as it constrains us once we
share it from Christ, is the strength by which we too can
live.

The strength to live in terms of God's love, and by
means of it, gives the capacity to live courageously.
Jesus was the 'Strong Son of God'; and his strength made
him a brave man. I speak here, not of physical strength—
for all I know, Jesus may not have been possessed of that;

and some have thought that his early death on the Cross indicates a physical exhaustion under all the pressures which had come upon him—I speak of moral strength, of spiritual strength, of the terrible strength of those who are meek. The Chinese Taoists like to talk about how much stronger may be a steady dripping of water than some violent torrent. Whatever we think of that saying, it is 'the magnitude of meekness', in Christopher Smart's lovely phrase, which confronts us in Jesus—and in his saints, too, where 'strength is made perfect in weakness', and 'things which are not' are shown to be mightier than 'things that are'. The Italians sometimes end a letter with the words, 'Forte, forte,' addressed to friends whom they would encourage. Encouragement means that we are made more courageous to face and accept as well as to will and to do. Jesus accepted the will of God; he was strengthened by the grace of God; he was brave before men because God was with him, even unto, even through, the death he must endure. His courage is contagious. 'Be strong and quit you like men', was the Maccabean cry; the follower of Christ, caught up into the courage of Jesus, is able to be strong in his strength and brave in his bravery. Life with God in Christ is courageous life, ready to stand firm against hatred, meanness, injustice, dirtiness, selfishness, wherever found. It can dare to be strong, as its Lord dared, because 'he that is with us is mightier than he that is against us'. How one wishes that the Christian Church today showed more of that courage—the willingness to love, and to add (if I may put it so), 'the consequences be damned'.

The life which is in Christ and which Christ is, is life in love. To the love which is Christ we are to devote an entire lecture; here I should wish only to make the point.

Sometimes I have remembered the way in which, many years ago, I heard Humphrey Beevor phrase the words of the Fourth Gospel: 'In the beginning was Love, and Love was with God, and Love was God. . . . All things were made through Love; without Love nothing was made that was made. In Love was life; and the life was the light of men; and the light (which was Love) shineth in darkness, yet the darkness overcame it not. . . . And Love was enfleshed and dwelt among us, full of grace and truth.'

Whatever you may think of that way of putting it, surely the truth about Christ is that he *is* embodied, enfleshed, en-manned Love, and the life which we live in communion with him is life in his love which is the love of God manifest and shed abroad. I well know the danger of sentimentalizing this; I shall warn against it, and guard against it, as we come to the end of these lectures. But I dare to think that we are in greater danger, these days, of *under*-sentimentalizing, despite all that is said about the looseness and the laxness of the 'new theo-logy' and the 'new morality'. Let us affirm boldly that conviction which Thornton Wilder in *The Bridge of San Luis Rey* put in these words: 'Love is the only survival, the only meaning.' Let us honestly acknowledge that we have been deficient in love, precisely because we have been deficient in life—we who are of the Church; while at the same time we acknowledge that the reverse is equally true: we have been deficient in life, precisely because we have been afraid, terribly afraid, to live in love. For love very often makes us look foolish; nobody much wants to be a fool, even 'for Christ's sake'. The respectability of the established churches, not only of the

Established Church, has got into us and quenched the fire of love in us. So we need, all the more courageously to live lives which risk themselves for love's sake, which is to say, for God's sake.

One of my old teachers said to me one day that a Christian *must* wear his heart on his sleeve, he *must* be vulnerable. The Christian is no stoic, who goes through life, and who lives, as if possessed by *apatheia*. He must feel and feel intensely. That can hurt; but the Lord whom we adore did not find Calvary and what preceded it a very comfortable and pleasant experience. Love is bound to be hurt, in a world which is not yet the Kingdom of God. But because the life in love is brave, is strengthened by God's own love, has a purpose to which it is dedicated without reserve, and knows itself to be built on the solid rock of authenticity or truth, it can face and accept the hurt. Yet 'hurt' is not the last word about the life which is Christ and which is ours in Christ.

I did not mention it in my list given earlier in this lecture, because I did not wish to anticipate what is the end-product of it all; now I come to that last word . . . it is 'joy'. The life of Jesus was marked by such joy that he could endure the cross which was in his path; the life of the Christian is filled also with a joy that the world itself can never take away. Baron von Hügel said that one of the reasons, he supposed, that Cardinal Newman cannot quite be called a 'saint' is that he did not possess that particular quality of life, that joy. I do not know much about Newman; it may be that von Hügel was wrong. However, I have no doubt at all that the great saints are joyous men and women; and above all I have no doubt that part of what attracted people to our Lord himself was the sheer joy that marked his life among them. One might even dare to say that Jesus was 'happy', if by this we mean the kind of blessedness which guards us from gloom, despair, hopelessness, and a pessimistic rejection of the world and of others.

Some of us, probably, are temperamentally (one might even say, physiologically) better equipped than others for happy moods and happy thoughts. But *all* of us, by virtue of our Christian commitment, can be delivered from steady gloom, blind despair, miserable hopelessness, and the readiness to reject this world and the people who live in it. It is too bad that the 'image' of the Church and of Christians which far too often we have managed to convey to the 'outsider', is one of sheer gloom and misery. It is a false image, we well know, and it is no worse than the kind of stupid 'cheer' which sometimes is associated with a certain type of parson. What a ghastly pair of images are these two, either unrealistic levity which cannot face things as they are, or a professional gloom which *The New Yorker* magazine in its cartoons associates with undertakers and hired pall-bearers. I may have utterly misread the gospels and totally failed to understand their central figure, but I must say that to me it seems that Jesus went through this world like a flaming fire, like one who burned with love, like one who wore our humanity as a royal garment, like one who rejoiced.

The life which our Lord brings to us is exactly the same as his own: it is true life, authentic life, real life, life with purpose, life with strength, life with courage, life in love. It is life in joy, too. For the God who sent him and who was in him, the God who got through to us in a decisive way by means of that same Jesus, is a God who himself is joy. In the biblical pictures, heaven is a banquet, not a funeral; it is a feast, not a fast; it is marked by 'joy and triumph everlasting'. Surely in us 'the powers of the age to come' should be reflected in a joy which is like that. 'Let us rejoice and be glad', for 'the Lord God omnipotent reigneth', and the joy which is in heaven is given freely to the sons of men.

4

The Love which Christ discloses

I⟶ is the Fourth Evangelist who seems to see most deeply into the mystery of the Love which is Christ and which Christ discloses. The synoptic writers, ordering the primitive oral traditions which conveyed the impression Jesus made upon those who during 'the days of his flesh' were his companions, seem to be content with telling us more about what 'the eye saw' or 'the ear heard'. The writer of the Fourth Gospel lets us know what 'entered into the heart of man', living in deepest communion with the risen Lord, to perceive and apprehend as the inner meaning of it all. Especially in the discourse at the Last Supper, in chapters thirteen to sixteen, and in the high priestly prayer, in chapter seventeen, we seem to be allowed almost to penetrate into the very heart of Jesus himself, as he sat with his 'little flock' to whom he had promised the Kingdom, and talked with them of the things that were his abiding concern, both for himself and for them. In the high priestly prayer itself, we who are Christians must feel that we are on holy ground, for this is Jesus' own self-dedication to the Father on behalf of those whom he loved, and with whom he would share the love of the Father for him, and his returning love for the Father, and the Father's purpose of love.

I confess that I find it very hard to speak about these things. For I cannot read or hear those sections of John without emotions so deep that they move me to tears.

They are a long development of what Dean Crossman's hymn calls 'my saviour's love for me'—and not for me only, but for the company of all Christian disciples, and beyond that for the whole world of men. You remember, I hope, George Tyrrell's words: that when he was prepared to give up his struggle with a narrow and intolerant ecclesiastical authority, he turned his thoughts to 'that strange Man on his cross', and how for him, the cross meant Jesus 'with his arms spread wide to embrace the whole of the *orbis terrarum*'. It seems to me that the Fourth Evangelist has seen and understood all this; and has expressed it with a directness and poignancy which readily explain why his gospel has been so much loved by Christians in every age. For however the writer may have modified and re-arranged the events he records, however different may be the traditions upon which he depends from those familiar to the synoptists, he has surely got to 'the heart of the matter'; and that heart is a heart of love, a burning charity which consumes all that is unlovely and hateful and selfish and wrong and false and untrue—a charity which is nothing other than the love of God made manifest in this supreme instance of human caring.

'Having loved his own which were in the world, he loved them unto the end. . . .' 'Love never faileth.' Here are two scriptural texts which sum up what Jesus' life is about, supremely what his passion and death are about. It is then to a consideration of that 'love of God which was in Christ Jesus our Lord' that we now shall turn.

The first thing that we may say of the love of God in Christ is that it establishes a relationship between persons. 'Only connect', Mr. E. M. Forster has said. Here is 'connection' in the most profound sense. As between human beings, the greatest of all needs is for deep and understanding relationship, the realization that we are knit together as brethren and the making actual in our doings of that realization. Paul Tillich talked a great deal about love as the establishment of unity; it is, he said, the true reconciliation of that which and those who seem to be separated one from the other. Unitive life, which is life in love, is established among us in our response to the Love which moved among us in Jesus. It is a deeper unity than the common affection or attraction of man to man, although it is not the denial of that affection or attraction but its coronation and completion, as also it is its correction and its rightful ordering. I have little or no patience with the kind of theological or homiletical talk which denigrates human love in order to exalt divine love, nor can I accept the sharp distinction between the love of *agape*, which is said to give and never to ask for response, and *eros* and *philia*, which are said to be the desire to receive or the experience of a sheer mutuality. As I read the story, the Love which is God and which was en-manned in Jesus does indeed give and give and give, but it yearns for response; it is desire in its fullest expression and it is mutuality to the degree that it brings into existence a community, a fellowship, a belonging-together, which is nothing short of the Kingdom of God.

But of course it is pre-eminently a Love that gives. It is a self-giving to another self who thereby and in response is brought also to give. That, I suppose, is why sexual union in faithful mutuality can be taken in scripture as a basic symbol for divine-human relations; that is why a wedding-feast is a fit intimation of the Kingdom where God reigns in love. The union of two human beings, bound together by promises of faithfulness, involves more than sensual desire although it certainly includes that. Chiefly it implies that one person gives himself in full surrender to another person who also gives in equally full surrender. Let us remember that in Christian thinking the estate of matrimony is a sacrament of a love that shares, a love that is very God himself. Jesus himself wished to be *with* his disciples, to share with them his life with the Father, to open to them his relationship of love to the Father, to enable in them his loyalty in love to the Father's purpose. And I do not hesitate to say that, at least on my reading of the gospels, Jesus wanted from those who are called his 'friends' a response which would involve a giving on their part too. His love evoked their answering love and welcomed that answer when it came.

The love which was in Christ was a compassionate love. It did not stand aloof but identified itself with men in their condition. The Society of Friends has always known this. I well remember, as if it were yesterday, a meeting of theologians in the College of Preachers in Washington, D.C., just after the second world war. In one of the intermissions, the American Quaker theologian, Rufus Jones, asked if he might say a few words to us. He told us about the children in certain parts of the world who were badly in need of milk and of clothing. 'I have this great concern on my heart', he said, as he asked us to do what we could to help feed and clothe those who were but recently children of an enemy nation. One knew that Jones was utterly identified with those needy folk; his 'concern' was not a remote interest but an immediate awareness, as if he himself shared their plight. You will remember that von Hügel once said that 'Christianity taught us to care . . .'. Caring, in this most profound sense of sharing with another in his sorrows as in his joys, is love in action; it is compassion such as Christ felt for the multitude when he saw them hungry in a desert place; it is the charity which itself becomes those for whom it has concern. 'The cup of cold water' is the sign of that compassion and its expressive instrument.

Love as brought to us in Christ is connection or relationship, it is a giving which awakens a responsive giving, it is fellow-feeling or compassion. It is also utter commitment. We have mentioned this already in speaking of true human love as the full surrender of one person to another, but it is worth our dwelling upon it a little more. For commitment is what redeems giving from being bare and chilly; we all know that 'the gift without the giver' is a poor thing. One often thinks that the enormous amount of assistance which has been granted by privileged nations to those less privileged, while we ought to give this and indeed for our own safety in the world must give it, has not infrequently been vitiated by a *de haut en bas* attitude, precisely because the heart and soul of the giver was not given with the gift. In personal relationships this is even more obviously true. One can sympathize with the Cockney woman who is reported to have said to the Lady Bountiful who came to the slum-dwelling with all her gifts, 'Don't go on saving your soul *on me*.' But Lady Bountiful was not even 'saving her soul'; she was just distributing from her plenty a largesse that irritated and annoyed even if in another sense it aided the recipients.

The commitment of oneself to another person may mean suffering. In our Lord this is poignantly demonstrated, for surely the greater part of his suffering was not physical at all, but the inner pain of seeing that those whom he loved so deeply and for whom he would give so much did not seem to want him; 'he was despised and rejected of men, a man of sorrows and acquainted with

D

grief'. And yet, and yet . . . in all the suffering which
commitment involves, something wonderful is released
The sheer goodness which is found there can break down
resistance, overcome prejudice, opens up avenues for
understanding, if not immediately then 'in the long run'
And God's 'run' is very long, for he has all time in which
to win a response. Since his love never fails, we are
permitted to entertain the faith that in this long run
despite the suffering which is felt by the divine Lover a
the rejection of his love, and even because of the suffering
when it is once seen for the utter compassion which i
exhibits and the total commitment which it presupposes
that love of his will one day hold all men, and the whole
world, captive by the chains of an answering 'amen' of
love. If this is not a possible faith, I for one could no
continue to be a Christian.

Again, the love which is in Christ Jesus is the love tha
understands. 'Father, forgive them, for they know not wha
they do.' So our Lord prayed. *They* did not know, bu
he did. He knew how the prejudice, hatred, and rejection
were not simple and sheer wickedness, but ignorance
misguided grasp of truth, impotence of will, and fear o
consequences. Pascal once said that men never sin se
happily as when they do it with what they take to be a
'good conscience'. That was true of those who sent ou
Lord to the cross. To think that people act in utter
malice, with no grain of good in them, is to deny th
great insight of a Thomas Aquinas—and, indeed, of al
Catholic moral theology—that there is nothing, literall
nothing, that is *malum in se*. The doctrine of creation
sometimes overlooked in our understandable stress o
the doctrine of redemption, should have guaranteed thi

insight. And the love which Christ is, in all its identification, its self-giving, its compassion, its commitment, is
the love which 'knows what is in man'; and knowing can
forgive.

Only God can forgive, for only God can really understand. But God in Christ forgives, because God in Christ
understands. The gracious pressure of that love upon us,
which forgives us despite our acknowledged unaccept-
ability, can awaken in us our own measure of forgiving-
ness. That is part of the secret of life with God in Christ . . .
to forgive until seventy times seven, and then to go on
forgiving. Forgiving love is directed towards the future,
which is why it is not immoral to forgive. It sees persons
in terms of what they have it in them to be; it understands
in the sense that it can grasp something of what it must
have been like to have lived in those circumstances,
under those threats, with those failures, in the context of
that situation. So it will not condemn; it will pardon. Of
course the past cannot be undone; it is the nature of the
past to remain fixed precisely because it *is* past. But the
future is open; there is more to come; there will be new
opportunities in new occasions. As I once put it, in a
book written long ago, the forgiving love of God enables us
to bear as a cross what we might have been obliged to
endure as a curse. In our own measure, too, it is given
to us to enable our fellows to live for the future, for what
they have it in them to be.

Our Lord 'knew what was in man'. Not only did he
know the depths of their sin, the twisted motives, the
misguided desires, and the wrong intentions; he also knew
that much deeper than these is the Love which made and
makes them, the Love which is God himself. His yearning
was to release that Love in them, so that it might flood

through their lives and make them new beings. Man is not radically sinful, for at his roots man is in the image of God. His sin is a disease, which can be cured and so the man made whole. That is why the love which we know in Christ is *hopeful* love, eager to find the faintest suggestion of response, ready to use each and every movement of good wherever and however that may be brought forth. Connecting, giving, sharing, committing, suffering, forgiving, hoping ... that is the love of God declared to us in Jesus Christ.

In James Baldwin's novel *Another Country*, there is a scene in which two men, Eric and Vivaldo, who are among the striking characters in a quite remarkable book, discover that they love one another. The circumstances are not such as would gain much social approval, for the two make their discovery during a homosexual relationship, although they themselves are not both of them homosexuals. In the scene to which I refer, there are these words, spoken of Vivaldo: 'He felt fantastically protected, liberated, by the knowledge that, no matter where, once the clawing day descended, he felt compelled to go, no matter what happened to him from now until he died, and even, or perhaps especially, if they should never lie in each other's arms again, there was a man in the world who loved him. All of his hope, which had grown so pale, flushed into life again. He loved Eric; it was a great revelation. But it was yet more strange and made for an unprecedented steadiness and freedom, that Eric loved him.'[1]

I think these words are very beautiful and that, whatever we may think about the circumstances in which they are uttered, they speak to a genuine and general

[1] *Another Country*, by James Baldwin (Michael Joseph).

human situation. The need to be protected, liberated, given hope, made steady and free, is an abiding human need. That need brings to a vivid focus, I believe, the actual human drive for life with another which will bring us out of the appalling solitude in which we feel lost and afraid. All our scientific inventions, all our modern comforts and conveniences, all the splendid new world which many think is now dawning, will never be able to provide men with the relationship in loving self-giving that can bring richness and colour to our lives and save us from triviality and frustration. We shall never understand what it is that brings men and women together in relationships that are, or are not, socially approved and accepted, until and unless we have seen the profound truth which, I think, Bruce Marshall once stated in words that at first may appear shocking and blasphemous: 'The man who rings the door-bell of a brothel is really seeking God.'

Purposely I have quoted an extreme statement of what I take to be terribly true. In any and every attempt, made by any and every human being, to do what, as we have said, Mr. E. M. Forster taught us to call 'connect'—that is, to be in a genuine and deep relationship with another—and in all the substitutes which humankind employ when they feel deprived of that mutuality in relationship, there is a quest for the Love which is of God and which is God. If Vivaldo could discover, in an 'illicit' relationship with another man, something of that meaning, who are we to say that God cannot and does not use very strange ways to reach into the human heart? Please understand that I am not here urging antinomian ideas or supposing that any and every relationship of love must be given our wholehearted approval. But I am saying that there is a danger that our over-moralistic condemnation may put us in the position of the Pharisee, and that Jesus himself was more generous and open to love wherever it was found, and in whatever unfortunate guise it might appear, than the severe legalist, the puritanical prude, and the shocked defender of bourgeois respectability.

It was of a human love, and that of a kind which society would condemn, that Baldwin wrote the words I have quoted. But human love, when it is real and involves genuine fidelity and self-giving, is a vehicle, a sign, and if you will, a sacrament, of the 'Love which moves the sun and the other stars'. And I think that the words which Vivaldo used may with real force be applied to the *divine*-human love of which the gospels are the record and witness. The love which loved us to the end, to death itself and through death itself, is the love that can give to men an even more certain protection, liberation, hope, steadiness, and freedom. The events surrounding our Lord's crucifixion, the loving surrender to what he took to be the Father's will, the tenderness of his care for his little flock coupled with the firmness of his resolve to see through to the bitter end the duty laid upon him: all this, for Christian faith, is a disclosure of the kind of love which is indeed what a popular song of my own youth called 'the sweet mystery of life'—sweet, yes, but also terrible in its splendour and triumphant over all manner of evil and selfishness and wrong.

Notice the words that Baldwin uses: protection, liberation, hope, steadiness, freedom. Do they not ring true in the mystery of the Love which for us men endured suffering, bore the cross, died in full surrender, *and* was validated and vindicated by what we call the resurrection?

Protection . . . not from the vicissitudes of daily life or from the risks we must take and the perils we must face, but protection from sheer stupidity and lack of meaning, from the appalling fear that our human best counts for nothing in this awful world where our lot is cast, from what the American Prayer Book describes as 'faithless fears and worldly anxieties'. Liberation . . . the glorious sense of release from those same fears, coupled with the open and grateful acceptance of things as they come to us in 'the sacrament of the present moment' (as Père Jean de Caussade put it); liberation from despair into expectation, so that we may indeed begin to live with that 'tip-toe expectancy' of which von Hügel spoke and to feel that we are moving in a world which, however strange and surprising, is yet a home and not a prison-house. Hope . . . which follows from that liberation and expresses that expectancy, in the confidence that however dreadful our past and however disturbing our present, we can look to a future which God who is Love has prepared for us, where sin, evil, and death shall be overcome and we shall know the joy of life in the Kingdom whose monarch is Love himself and whose only law is the royal law of love. Steadiness . . . and see again how the words are building up . . . steadiness, which means a confidence and a stability in our thinking and doing, a strengthening and a firming-up, enabling us to quit ourselves like men and go about our business of human living with purpose and strong intent, rather than with stumbling and bumbling, with faltering and weakening, as and when things get difficult and we must face the 'changes and chances of this mortal life'. And freedom . . . the chance to be the freemen of the world, made free in Christ with a freedom that only a loving Father can give. All these are the consequence of

love and of our 'being in Love' (with a capital 'L', you
notice) which is the true meaning of 'being in Christ' and
hence of 'being in God' who is in Christ.

But our own loving is so weak, our direction in loving so
easily mistaken, our capacity to love in the right way so
limited, that each and every one of us can only say with
W. H. Auden in *Canzone*, that 'all must be forgiven, *out of
love*, that all must be forgiven, *even love*'. It is the love
which is exhibited to us and poured out upon us in Jesus
Christ, incarnate, crucified, and regnant, which will forgive us, as it is that same love which 'knowing our infir-
mities' will pardon and empower our poor loving, and
through the union of his great love with our stumbling
little love will make us into true lovers. St. Augustine
prayed that God would 'order his love'; so must we.
While this re-ordering and refreshing and enabling of us
is indeed very mysterious, it is not too unlike something
we all know quite well. In our intercourse with our
friends, in our human relationship with those whom we
seek to love and whom we do love so far as we are able,
we have experienced the gracious influence of the life of
the other, who through his loving of us has given us new
courage, new power to love, and new joy in loving. In
somewhat the same way, we may dare think, the gracious
influence of Christ, which is the grace of God in him,
enters our lives as we try to open ourselves to him. And
behold, we are made new, we are given strength, we find
joy; we are, in fact, released from our pettiness and
enlarged in our loving. We can go about our daily tasks
with a song in our hearts and a lightness in our steps,
because we have been caught up into, and made partici-
pants of, the Love which will never let us go.

I should be sorry, I suppose, that I have ended this lecture on a homiletic note; the lecture seems to have become a sermon. But I do not apologize. We are thinking this week of the deepest and truest assertions of our faith and how can one do otherwise than *proclaim* that faith? A sermon is a proclamation of the generous love of God in Christ, or it is not a Christian sermon; and no continued contemplation of the Lord Christ can end without passing over into a glad proclamation of him as the *way*, which is to say the *truth* about our existence and the *life* which is offered to us in him. We do not need to seek longer for the *way* in which we can walk with confidence, steadiness, hope, assurance; as St. Augustine said, the way has come to us in Jesus. It is for us to walk in it, and discover that it is in very fact the way of love.

E

5

He in whom the Word was made Flesh

A RATHER vocal school of theologians in the United States
who have announced fairly recently 'the death of God'
have also given currency to the idea that in the contem-
porary world there is no possibility of faith, in any ultimate
sense, for there is nothing and no one to whom one might
surrender in total trust. They have also told us that hope
is impossible, for in a world which is entirely describable
in terms of science, however sophisticated, there is nothing
for which one could hope, all genuine novelty having been
excluded by definition and any glorious consummation
being ruled out from the start. What is left, they tell us
is the possibility and indeed the necessity of love. This they
define as open-ness to others, willingness to give oneself for
the best good of those others, and the desire to enter as
deeply as possible into relationships of mutual concern
and caring.

I do not myself agree with these theologians, whose
announcement of 'the death of God' seems to me very
premature. Of course it is true that many of the idols
which for long years have pointed towards but more
disastrously have also pointed away from God, have been
and are being smashed. The 'god' who intervenes in
the world to arrange things for our private comfort or
convenience, the 'god' who is the defender of the privilege
of social groups and national policies, the 'god' whose
existence was simply to provide what Harry Emerson

Fosdick once called 'a cosmic bellhop' for the human race; that 'god' or those 'gods' are indeed quite dead. But then that 'god' never was alive. He existed only as a projection of human desires, although the fact that a projection was made was, I think, indicative of some deeply felt sense of there being Someone or Something ultimately real, with whom men could be in relationship. The real God, the only God who is real, is not dead; he is alive now as he has been in the past and as he will ever be, working in and through this world towards the achievement of ever greater good which is to be in 'widest commonalty' shared.

Furthermore, I do not myself think that faith is an impossibility or hope an absurdity, since I cannot sub-scribe to the kind of 'cosmic impiety' (to use a fine phrase once employed by Bertrand Russell as a criticism of John Dewey's too man-oriented view of the world) which fails to see the deep grounding of human experience in the structure of things and in the dynamic which moves through things. But if faith and hope were impossible and only love were left, I should still wish to ask the question: 'Does love have any ontological significance?' Indeed, it may well be that the insistence made by these American thinkers on the centrality of love and its utter necessity can provide for them a 'little door', which like that in Dante's *Divine Comedy* will give access eventually to deeper and higher truth. For what kind of world is this in which we live, where love *is* a possibility and a necessity? What sort of world is it in which men and women can give themselves to others, identify themselves with the good of others, and show that concern and care which these theologians both commend and affirm to be an open option for human beings?

I should suppose that such a world is very different from one in which love is not a possibility at all, where the claim for its necessity is ridiculous, and where nobody in his senses would for a moment wish to open his life to the lives of other people. If love be all that these theologians think it to be, then the world in which such love is seen and known, experienced and reverenced, is a world which cries out for explanation—and so far as I can see, the only explanation which will be adequate carries with it the conviction that as love is the best and finest thing in our experience, so also is it the deepest and most real thing in the cosmos as a whole. Deep down, high up, all through this world, despite every appearance to the contrary, love must in some sense be 'sole sovereign lord'; or else love is an illusion and loving is an absurdity.

The reason that some of us are greatly attracted to what in North America is called 'process-philosophy', based on the thought of Whitehead but influenced by many other thinkers and writers, is precisely here. It seems to us that this way of looking at experience and understanding the world does in fact provide some cosmic grounding for the affirmation of love. Although that philosophy does not take its origin from the religious experience of men, but rather from an attempt to understand the wider and more general experience of the human race, as well as the implications of scientific discovery and the patent fact of emergence in the world of nature, history, and human life, it offers a kind of metaphysical setting into which the assurances of the Christian about the centrality of 'the love of God which was in Christ our Lord' can be fitted without serious distortion. It is my own conviction that the kind of re-conception of Christian faith which is so necessary in our time can best be accomplished with the use of that philosophy, rather than with some other popular alternatives such as the existentialism of Heidegger or the idealism of Tillich.

I say all this because I wish in this last lecture to speak of Jesus as that Man in whom 'the Word was made flesh'. In other words, I wish to bring all that has been said in earlier lectures, to bear upon the perennial Christian affirmation that God acted in Jesus in a supreme and definitive manner so far as mankind is concerned. For the light which we have been given about the nature and destiny of man, the world in which we live, and the quality of the divine reality we call God; the life which Jesus both lived in his days in the flesh in Palestine and still continues to impart to those who are caught up by his influence and feel themselves bound to him in discipleship and obedience; the love which in Jesus is shown to be the deepest truth about God and the intended truth about man; all these lead on to the common Christian conviction, expressed once for all in the words of the Fourth Evangelist, that the Word which from the beginning— that is, in principle—is the self-expressive activity of God, has been en-manned in the Man Jesus: 'In the beginning was the Word and the Word was with God and the Word was God. . . . And the Word was made flesh and dwelt among us, full of grace and truth.'

You may recall that in an earlier lecture I referred briefly to Whitehead's concept of 'importance'. That concept provides a starting-point for our discussion of the significance of Jesus Christ as Word-made-flesh. What do we mean by 'importance'? What is suggested to us when we call something 'important'? I suggest that we get at the notion by examining the way in which each of us tries to make sense of his own experience. Most of the

time, we shall admit, we go along in a more or less mono-
tonous way: we rise at a certain hour, we have breakfast,
we engage in our several duties, we have a break for coffee
in mid-morning, we return some time in early afternoon
for luncheon, we chat with our friends, we may go for a
walk or engage in playing some game or other, we have
tea later in the afternoon, perhaps we do some more work,
we have dinner followed by serious or desultory conver-
sation, we go to bed. That is the way life goes on, day in
and day out, with the odd Sunday or holiday or the
journey up to London. None of these things in and of
themselves will give us the key to the sense which we
make of our life; they are 'the trivial round, the common
task' which we accept because we must or because we
have at some point chosen to live in that fashion. But
there are other moments, special moments, which have
special importance. A tragic occurrence, the arrival of
our fiancée, some particular new duty which makes
extraordinary demands upon us, a great man whom we
meet . . . here are examples of important moments which
relieve the triviality of ordinary existence. I suppose that
somewhere along the line, in the lives of all of us, there
is *something* which has this quite special importance for
us. It is this something which becomes, however dimly
we may articulate it, 'the master-light of all our seeing';
it is in terms of this something that we begin to find that
our life has a meaning.

In the world at large, too, there are happenings,
persons, odd juxtapositions of people and circumstances,
etc., which have importance. It is these, taken as making
an unusual impact upon the course of events, which
become the key to whatever sense we can make of a

nation's history, a party's programme, a culture's development. In other words, our experience is not really on a uniformitarian level, if I may put it so; it has a certain variety; there are 'ups' and 'downs', high points and low points; there are particular occasions when somehow we seem to see more clearly 'what it is all about' and are able to say, as Robert Frost remarks in a little poem about a single choice once taken, 'and *that* has made the difference'.

In some such context of history and experience the life of Jesus Christ, and supremely the events of the last days of that life, are to be seen. Let me put it in more theological language. The God-man relationship, like the God-world relationship, is a continuing fact. No man at any time is without that relationship, however dimly he may understand it or even if he refuses to recognize its existence at all. No one can escape his being in and of the world; and that means that no one can escape his being in relationship with the dynamic reality which binds the world into a unity, energizes through it, and moves it on towards the future and its possibilities. But at one given point, in one particular Man, there is an intensification of the relationship, a fullnesss and adequacy not common but special. And that point occurs by a mysterious inter-penetration in which a whole constellation of causes comes to a focus: the drive in the natural order, the historical movement in a given place and among a given people, the response made to these pressures by the 'person in the midst', and the response made to *his* response by others around him and after him. Here is an *event* in a very rich sense of the word. The initiating cause is in the cosmos itself, so to say; or better put, it is in the divine agency which works in the cosmos to secure the satisfaction of its desire for greater good. God comes first, as

Christians have always said. But there is also response; the person himself, the genuinely human agent, has his part to play; and this means that although God comes first, man co-operates and participates, freely and of his own desire. Then others, caught up into the situation, feel its influence upon them and seek to respond in their own way and to enter into the complex event so that it is re-enacted, at a second step, in their own lives. So it is that the fellowship of response—the community of obedience, of discipleship, of love and emulation, of adoration—comes into existence, knit into one 'bundle of life' by engagement with the initiating movement of God in the life of that one Man in whom a full response was made to that movement.

I have been describing, in very abstract terms, what the New Testament as a whole tells us happened in the life of Jesus Christ and the days of the primitive Church. This is the given fact; and as Whitehead remarked in *Religion in the Making*, 'it is for Christians', considering the given fact, 'to discern the meaning'. They have sought to do so; the whole history of Christian theology, in all its splendour and in all its foolishness, is the story of their attempt to discern the meaning. What is the significance of this important moment in history, in the world, in the cosmos? The Christian answer is that here, in some supreme and decisive manner, the nature of God, and his way of acting—his agency—in the world, are disclosed in a concrete human life. 'The Word was made flesh.'

That 'en-fleshing', or better, that 'en-manning', is seen in the total life of the Man in whom it took place. From his birth, through his youth and manhood, as these are reflected for us in the gospels, the Word is 'taking flesh'. But it is obvious that it is in the last days, in Passion and

Holy Week as our church-year puts it, and in the sequence of events which followed in Easter and Pentecost, that the total meaning comes into vivid focus. Not the crucifixion without the resurrection, not the resurrection without the crucifixion; but the Cross seen in the light of the victory which Easter declares, and Easter seen as the vindication of the triumph of love over hate, of good over evil, of light over darkness, of life over death; this is the Christian reading of it. God is involved in all of it; he participates in all of it; he is revealed in all of it for what he *is* and in what he *does*. This is why we do well to meditate much on those 'mighty acts by which God has given to us life and immortality'. Passion Week and Holy Week, with their consequences in Eastertide through the ascension and Whitsunday, give us the key to an understanding of what is uniquely important in the whole life of Jesus; and Jesus' life, as being itself important, is the key to what God is and what God is doing.

I do not intend in this lecture to attempt to work out a christology. This is not the occasion for such an exercise; and in any event, I have already attempted in a large book to suggest how the person and work of Christ can be seen in the light of process-thought (*The Word Incarnate*, Nisbet, 1959). What I wish to do, in the remaining minutes of this last lecture, is to insist that it is time that we Christians took with *utmost* seriousness some of the implications of the central affirmations about Jesus which are summed up theologically in the doctrine of the person and work of Christ. I say 'about time', because I think that we have failed in a good deal of our thinking to give our full recognition to these implications.

There are three of them, in particular, about which I shall speak: (1) the necessity for seeing Love, and not some concept such as aseity or absolute power—for seeing sheer Love as the central and crucial symbol for our thought of God; (2) the need for seeing men, not in isolation from the life of Jesus, but as intimately and directly related to him—in other words, and in the negative sense, the need for *not* seeing Jesus in some imagined uniqueness which makes him, presumably for what we take to be his greater glory, utterly different from and alien to those whom he was willing to call his brethren; and (3) the need for re-conceiving the whole Christian 'thing' in the light of those two prior needs— or briefly, re-shaping our understanding of Christianity so that it is in accord with God as nothing other and nothing less than supreme Love, and also in accord with a view of man as so much made in the image of God, so much God's child, so much the brother of Jesus, that our notion of the meaning of sin and redemption is no longer drawn from law-courts or ancient master-slave relations or contractual arrangements, but instead is grounded in relationships of love, in the failure to love, and in the restoration of men to love. The whole point of the events which we are commemorating in these days is that God is indeed Love and as Love manifest in his Son; that men are created to be lovers and have in them already and always the working of that Love which is God himself; and that the Christian reality—church, worship, prayer, action, and the rest—is the enabling of men to actualize, by the influence of the love which is in Christ, their capacity to love and their need to love and their joy in loving.

Before we consider these three points, there is one prior remark to be made. I hope you see that I have protected what I am about to say and what in these

:ctures I have continually been saying from the charge of
sentimental and maudlin disregard of the hardnesses of
fe. I have protected it because I have insisted, again
nd again, that it is that *kind* of love which we contem-
late during Passion Week and Holy Week that is at the
eart of things. The love of God in Christ as manifested
a his suffering, death, and rising-again is no easy senti-
nent; it is a devastating love, 'more terrible than an
rmy with banners', stronger than the rivers which would
:ek to drown it, ready when need be to make almost
ntolerable demands and require almost insupportable
acrifice. This is no Hollywood cheapness, no pleasant
miability, no shoddy sentimental emotion. It is *strong*
ove, seen in the 'strong Son of Man'. I cannot think that
nyone who has looked at a crucifix and has imagined that
ver it are the words which before the bombing of St.
aul's were indeed the accompaniment of the represen-
ation of Christ's passion behind the old high altar: *Sic
Deus dilexit mundum*—I cannot imagine anyone with that
ision thinking that the Love which is God, which was
n-manned in Christ, which is the secret heart of every
nan's existence and the answer to his need, which is
) be made actual in the lives of all God's children, is
omething cheap, easy, or sentimental. No . . . a thousand
mes 'No'.

So we turn to the first of our needs, the taking of Love
s the central and abiding symbol for the nature of God
nd his activity. I can think, at the moment, of only one
ook of Anglican divinity which has sought to do just
nis, with the seriousness and consistency that I am asking.
'hat book is now long forgotten, I suppose; it is Father
. L. Strong's work *The Incarnation of God*, written by a
emarkable priest of the Oxford Mission Brotherhood in

India and published by Longmans Green as long ago as 1920. Doubtless there are other books, but I suspect there are few which are so thoroughgoing and vigorous. I commend Father Strong's study to you, not because I agree with all of it but exactly because it is written from the conviction that God is Love and Love is God. But let me develop the point in my own way.

All too frequently the symbol for God which is actually operative in our minds is drawn from the realm of sheer power. God is the potentate, the ruler 'in might', even the divine despot. How disastrous this has been to Christian theology! how many needless problems it has created! how it has made nonsense of man's freedom in relation to God's grace! There is no need to elaborate; what is needed is a complete jettisoning of all conceptions of power in God which are irreconcilable with the charity which is God himself. 'His nature and his name is Love', says Wesley's hymn. Let us accept this and think always in this way. And if God's deepest reality is indeed Love, then we can have nothing to do with basic ideas of God which portray him as the 'unmoved mover', the self-sufficient 'first cause', even the inert 'ground of being'. If he is really Love, then he is *always in relationship*: and if he is always in relationship, he is affected by what happens in the world. What goes on makes a *difference* to him; one could say, with due qualifications, makes a difference *in* him. He is distinct from his creation but he is never separated from it; he dwells in it, works through it, is affected by it, knows its anguish as he knows its joy. He cannot be impassible; although his capacity to bring good from evil, truth from error, beauty from ugliness, love from hate, assures him and us of his triumphant overcoming, in his own life and in the world too, of all

1at would make for evil, error, ugliness, and hate. But
oes this not mean 'suffering in God'? It does. 'There
as a cross in the heart of God before there was one on
'alvary', wrote an early twentieth-century American
1eologian—I think it was C. A. Dinsmore of Yale Uni-
ersity, but I do not know where and when he wrote it.
ut 'suffering in God' is always to be seen in the light of
'alvary *and* Easter; it is real compassion, but it is real
ictory too. As we have noted before, no Christian dare
)ok at Calvary without seeing it in the glory of Easter,
ut alternatively he dare not see Easter as if it were not
1e vindication and validation of the suffering of Calvary.

One might say much more about this first necessity,
ut we must hasten on to the second. We need to revise
ur doctrine of man so that the Incarnation is seen as
1e truth about him as well as the truth about Jesus,
lthough in vastly different degree; we need also to see
1e Atonement as the real at-one-ment between God as
ove and man who is made to be a lover, given the
1pacity to love, and is himself a place where divine love
 ceaselessly at work. This is at-one-ment of man with
imself, so that he can accept himself as he is and for what
e is, as Paul Tillich has taught us. It is at-one-ment
f man with his fellows, so that he can accept them in
pen charity as they are and for what they are. It is at-
ne-ment of man with God, so that in fellowship with
ove he can become a lover, a co-creator with God (as
Vhitehead once dared to put it) in the wider and wider
eation of occasions and means of love and for love.
nce we have understood this, we shall be obliged to go
1rough our hymnals and our liturgies and strike out sub-
1ristian, that is to say, unloving, ways of speaking of
od and man in relationship, of God's way of relating

himself to man and man to himself, of God's reconciliatic
of man to himself and to his fellows. Seen in the ligh
which streams from Calvary, man is indeed 'the dea
child of God's love', not a slave or a worm or a tot
mass of corruption and evil. One wonders how it ha
been possible for good Christian men to think and wri
in that horrible way about the brethren of the Son of Go
I am not minimizing the exceeding sinfulness of sin, ne
am I suggesting that man needs only a pat on the should
and a word of encouragement to become what in God
intention he always is; the fact of our Lord's passion a
death make such a notion absurd, not to say dishones
I only plead for our placing all our talk about sin a
sinfulness in a broader context, with a deeper insight in
our brotherhood with our Lord; I only ask that we reco
nize that we are made to be lovers, that in fact we a
frustrated and impotent lovers, and that we need to l
freed so that we can become the true lovers God wou
have us be, after the pattern and in the grace of his Sc
who is the great Lover.

Finally, the need for a re-conception of our Christia
enterprise in the light of these two. Already I have spoke
of the necessity for re-working our thought about sin a
atonement. Need I add other instances? Is the Chu
really a society of lovers en-graced by him who is Lo
Incarnate? Does our worship reflect that truth of th
Church's nature? Are our services such that this
plainly stated and clearly taught? So one could go o
But I shall not do so. I shall close by saying only that
my judgement *this* is the new reformation about which v
have heard so much: that in our theology, our worshi
our institutional life, our notion of Christian moralit
our understanding of Christian duty, our grasp of t

Christian mission in the world, in all these things and indeed in *everything*, we shall become more and more vividly aware of the chief Christian conviction. That conviction has to do with the divine charity in action, in Christ, known to us in our own self-commitment. It is a conviction which no one in our time has put more beautifully than T. S. Eliot:

> The dove descending breaks the air
> With flame of incandescent terror
> Of which the tongues declare
> The one discharge from sin and error.
> The only hope, or else despair
>   Lies in the choice of pyre or pyre—
>   To be redeemed from fire by fire.
> Who then devised the torment? Love.
> Love is the unfamiliar Name
> Behind the hands that wove
> The intolerable shirt of flame
> Which human power cannot remove.
>   We only live, only suspire
>   Consumed by either fire or fire.[1]

[1] 'Little Gidding' in *Four Quartets*, by T. S. Eliot (Faber & Faber).